GRAPHIC SCIENCE

THE DYNAMIC WORLD OF CHEMICAL REACTIONS

WITH MAX AXIOM SUPER SCIENTIST®

by Agnieszka Biskup

illustrated by Cynthia Martin and Barbara Schulz

Consultant:
Leslie Flynn, PhD
Science Education, Chemistry
University of Minnesota
Twin Cities Campus

CAPSTONE PRESS
a capstone imprint

Graphic Library is published by Capstone Press,
1710 Roe Crest Drive, North Mankato, Minnesota 56003.
www.capstonepub.com

Library of Congress Cataloging-in-Publication Data
Biskup, Agnieszka.
  The dynamic world of chemical reactions with Max Axiom, super scientist / by Agnieszka
Biskup ; illustrated by Cynthia Martin and Barbara Schulz.
    p. cm.—(Graphic library. Graphic science)
  Summary: "In graphic novel format, follows the adventures of Max Axiom as he explores
the science of chemical reactions"—Provided by publisher.
  Includes bibliographical references and index.
  ISBN 978-1-4296-4772-4 (library binding)
  ISBN 978-1-4296-5635-1 (paperback)
  1. Chemical reactions—Comic books, strips, etc.—Juvenile literature. I. Martin, Cynthia,
1961–ill. II. Schulz, Barbara (Barbara Jo), ill. III. Title. IV. Series.
  QD501.B677 2011
  541'.39—dc22   2010000557

Designer
Alison Thiele

Media Researcher
Wanda Winch

Cover Artists
Tod G. Smith and Krista Ward

Production Specialist
Laura Manthe

Colorist
Matt Webb

Editor
Christopher L. Harbo

Photo illustration credits: Shutterstock/Natalia Klenova, 6; Orca, 12, 13

Printed in the United States of America in Eau Claire, Wisconsin.
120116
010170R

TABLE OF CONTENTS

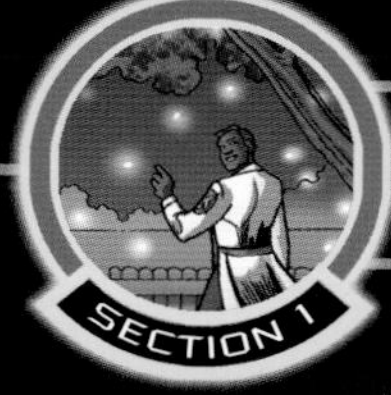
SECTION 1

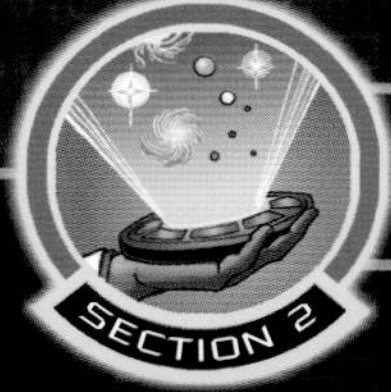
SECTION 2

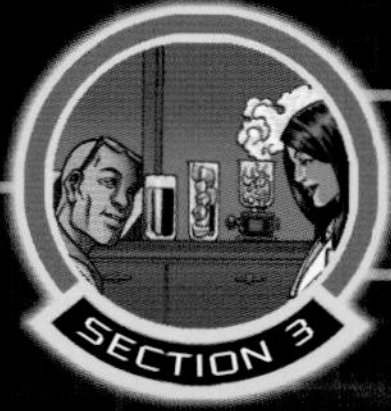
SECTION 3

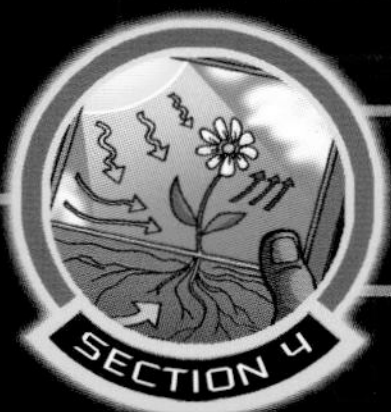
SECTION 4

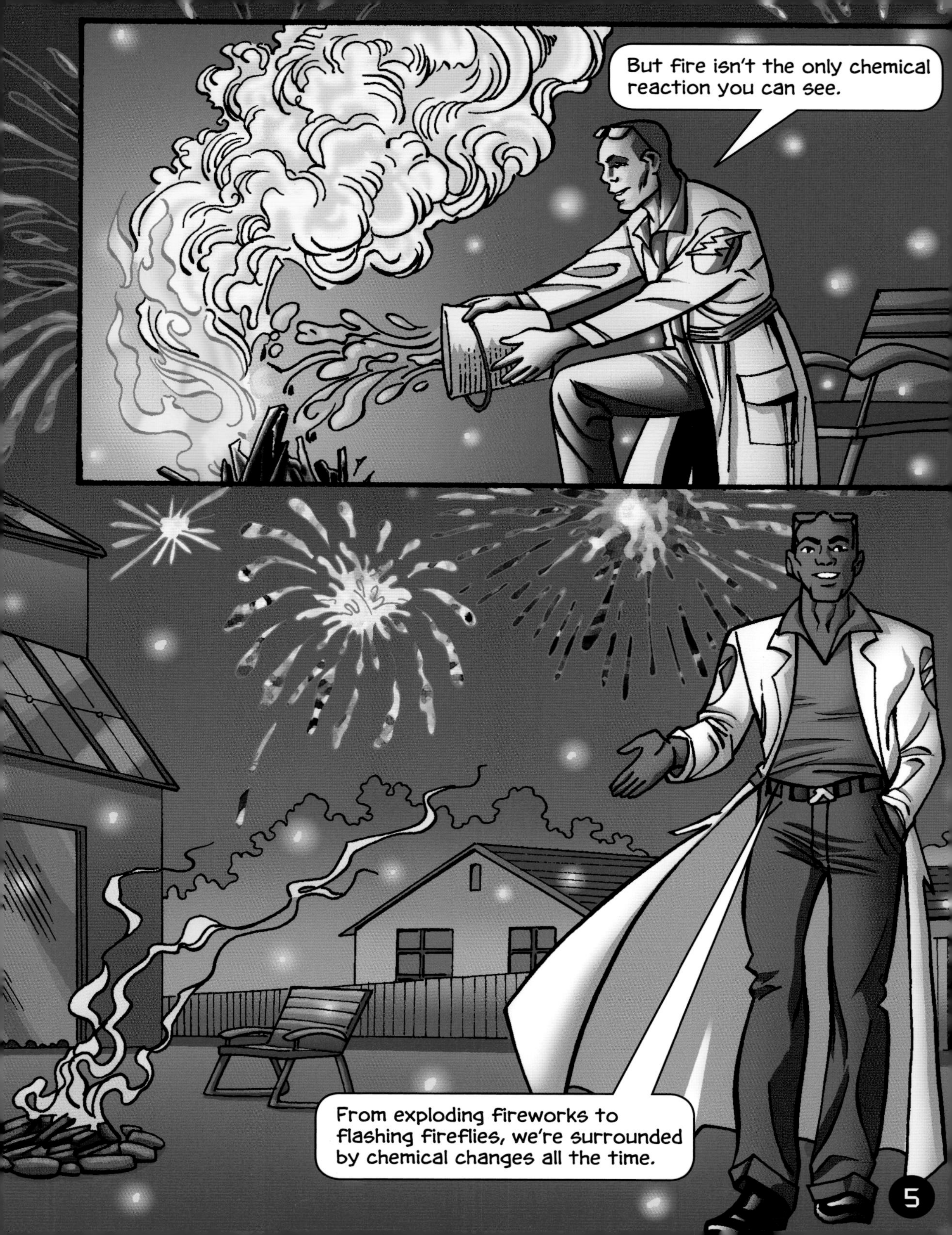
But fire isn't the only chemical reaction you can see.
From exploding fireworks to flashing fireflies, we're surrounded by chemical changes all the time.

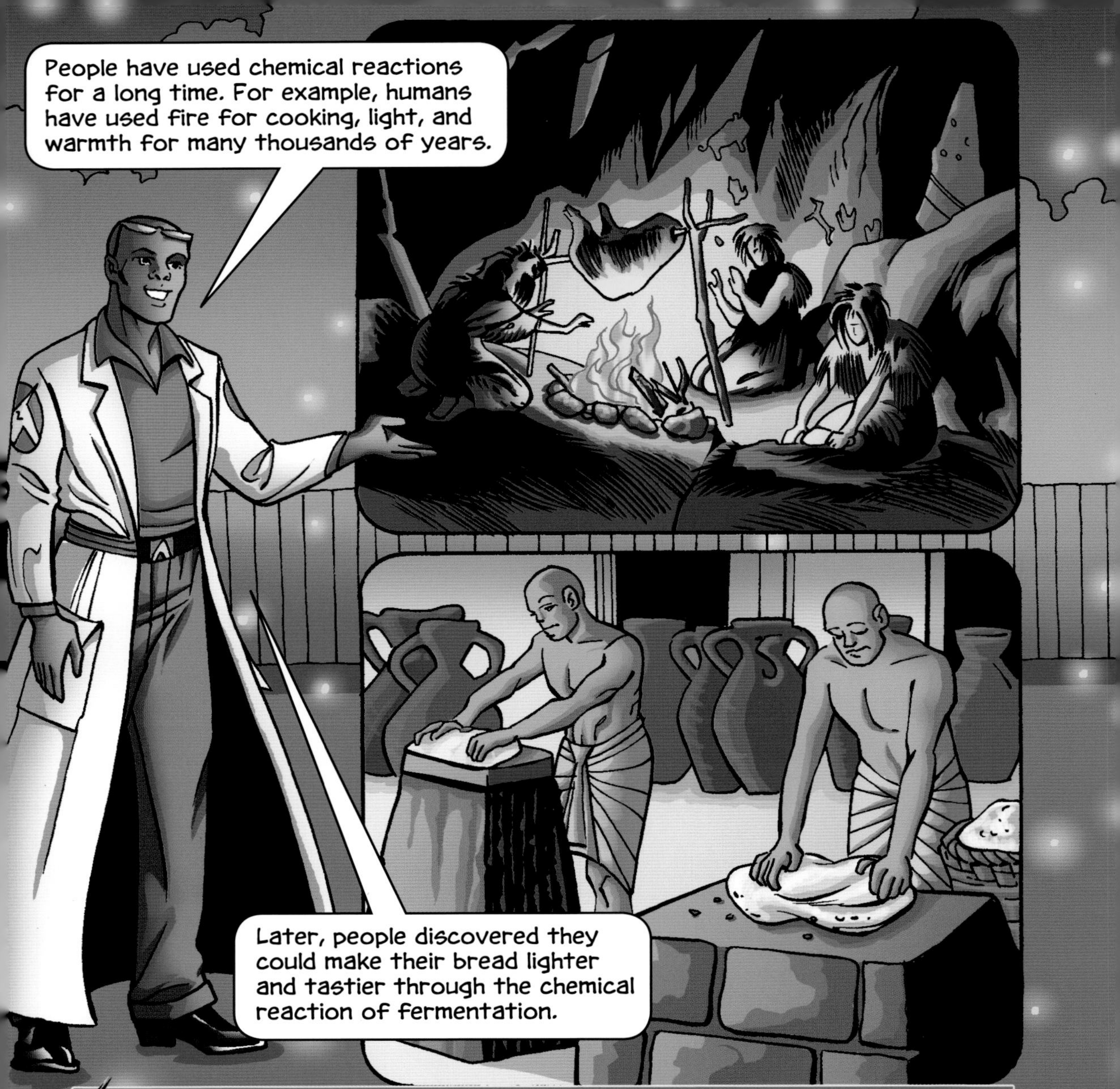
People have used chemical reactions for a long time. For example, humans have used fire for cooking, light, and warmth for many thousands of years.
Later, people discovered they could make their bread lighter and tastier through the chemical reaction of fermentation.

FERMENTATION

ACCESS GRANTED: MAX AXIOM

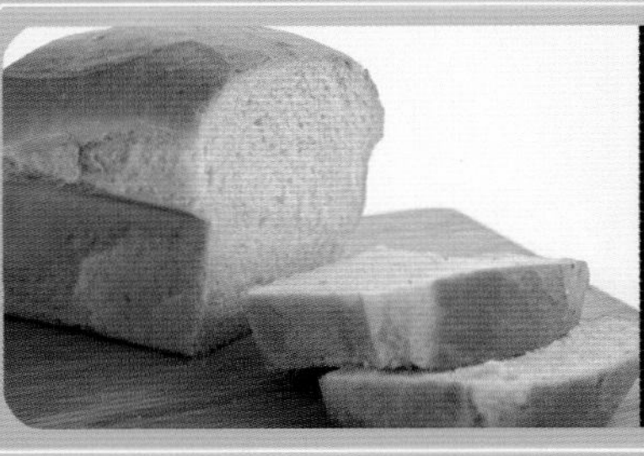

Fermentation can be used to produce various foods and beverages. It results when bacteria or yeast digest simple sugars. This digestion process gives off carbon dioxide gas and ethyl alcohol. It is the release of carbon dioxide gas that makes bread dough rise.

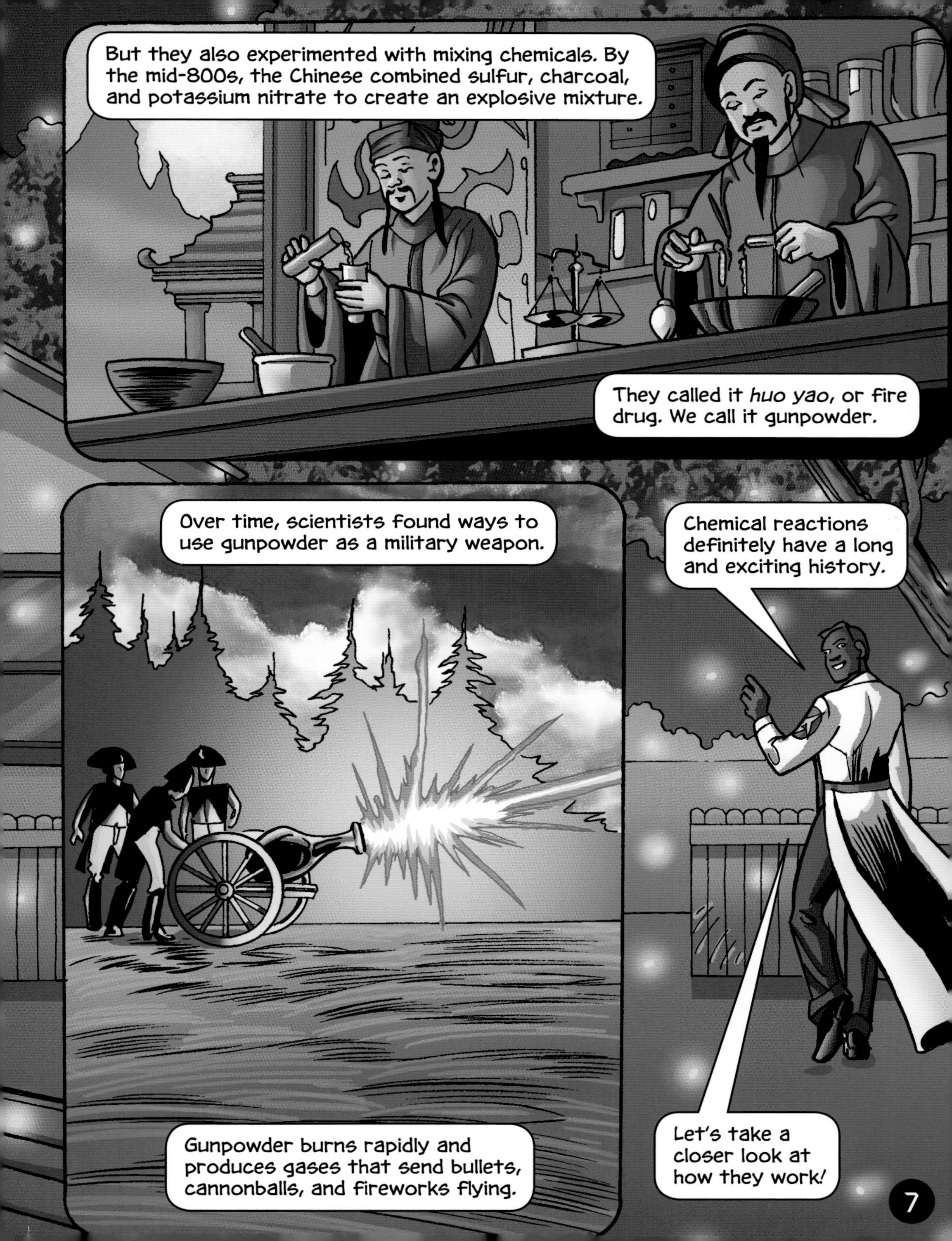

But they also experimented with mixing chemicals. By the mid-800s, the Chinese combined sulfur, charcoal, and potassium nitrate to create an explosive mixture.
They called it *huo yao*, or fire drug. We call it gunpowder.
Over time, scientists found ways to use gunpowder as a military weapon.
Gunpowder burns rapidly and produces gases that send bullets, cannonballs, and fireworks flying.
Chemical reactions definitely have a long and exciting history.
Let's take a closer look at how they work!

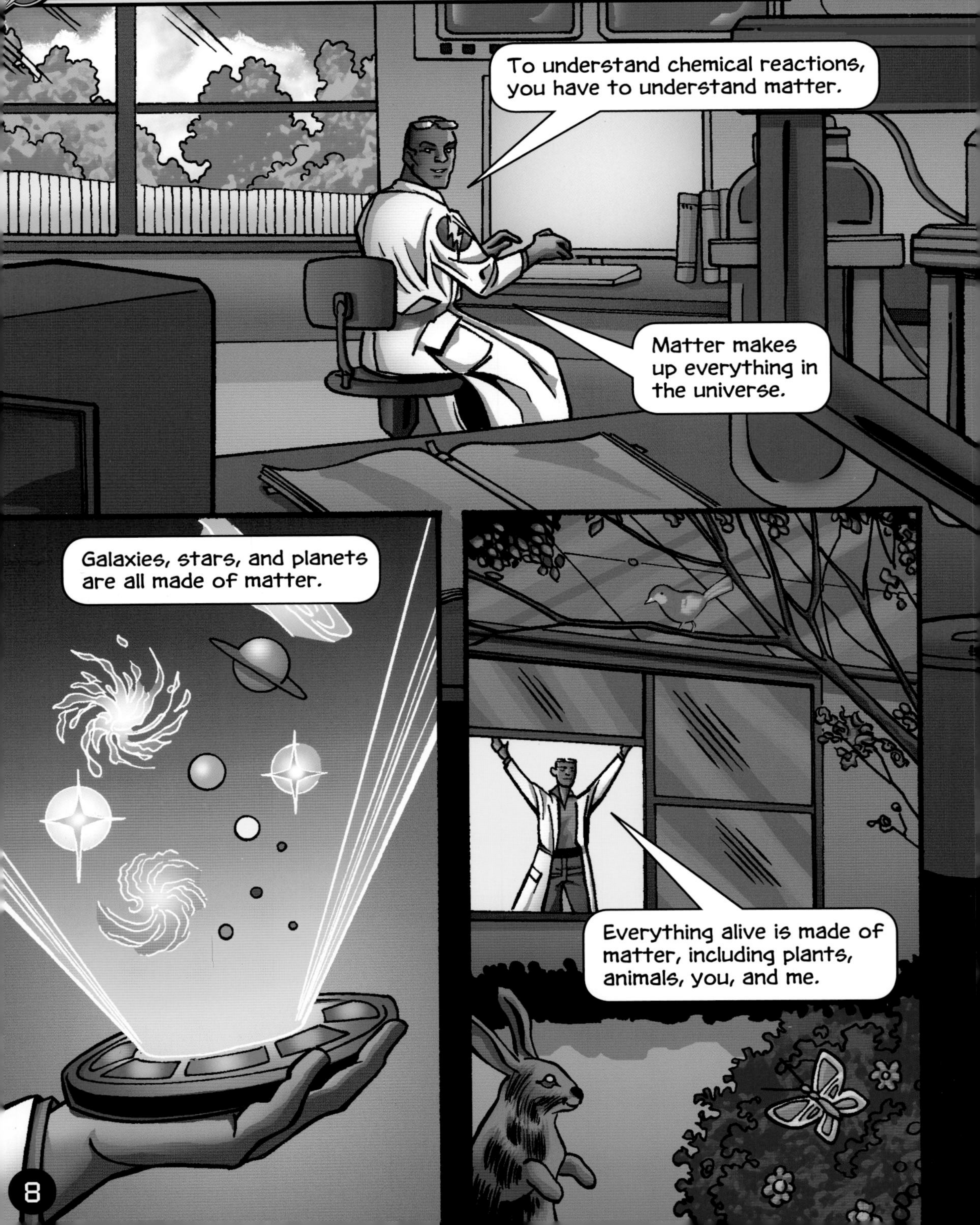
To understand chemical reactions, you have to understand matter.
Matter makes up everything in the universe.
Galaxies, stars, and planets are all made of matter.
Everything alive is made of matter, including plants, animals, you, and me.

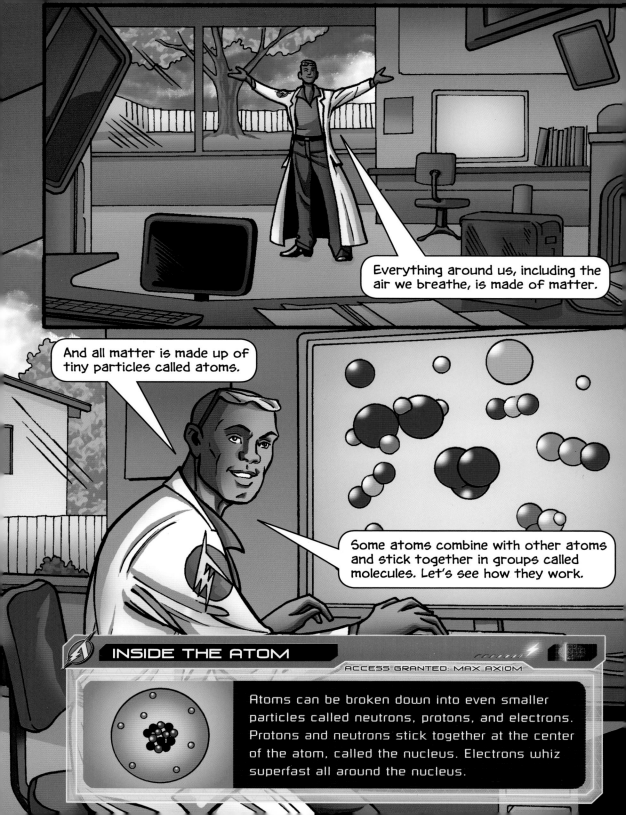

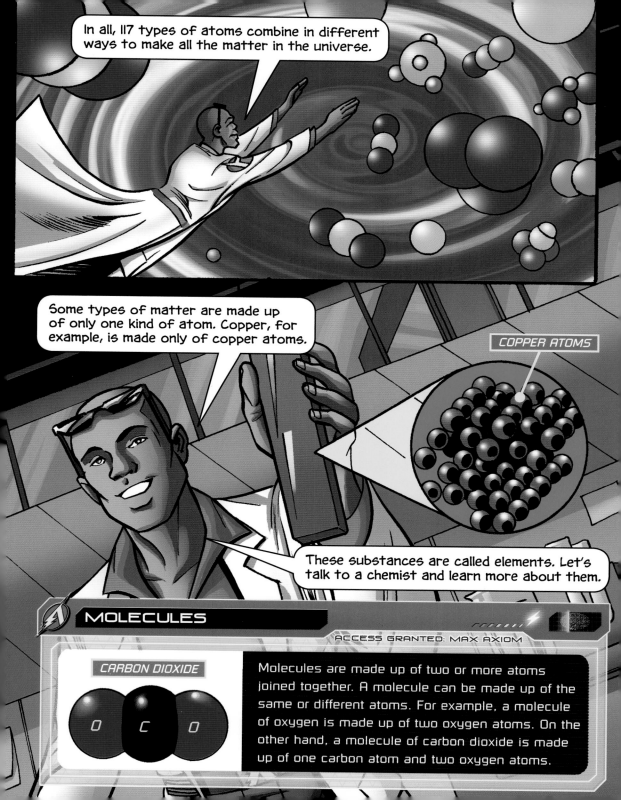

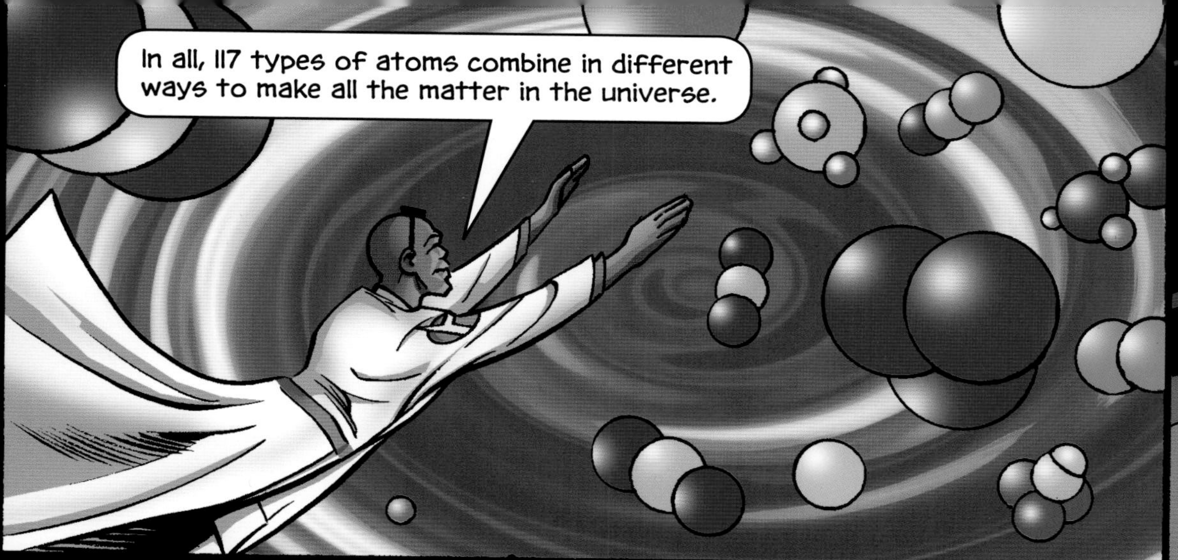
In all, 117 types of atoms combine in different ways to make all the matter in the universe.

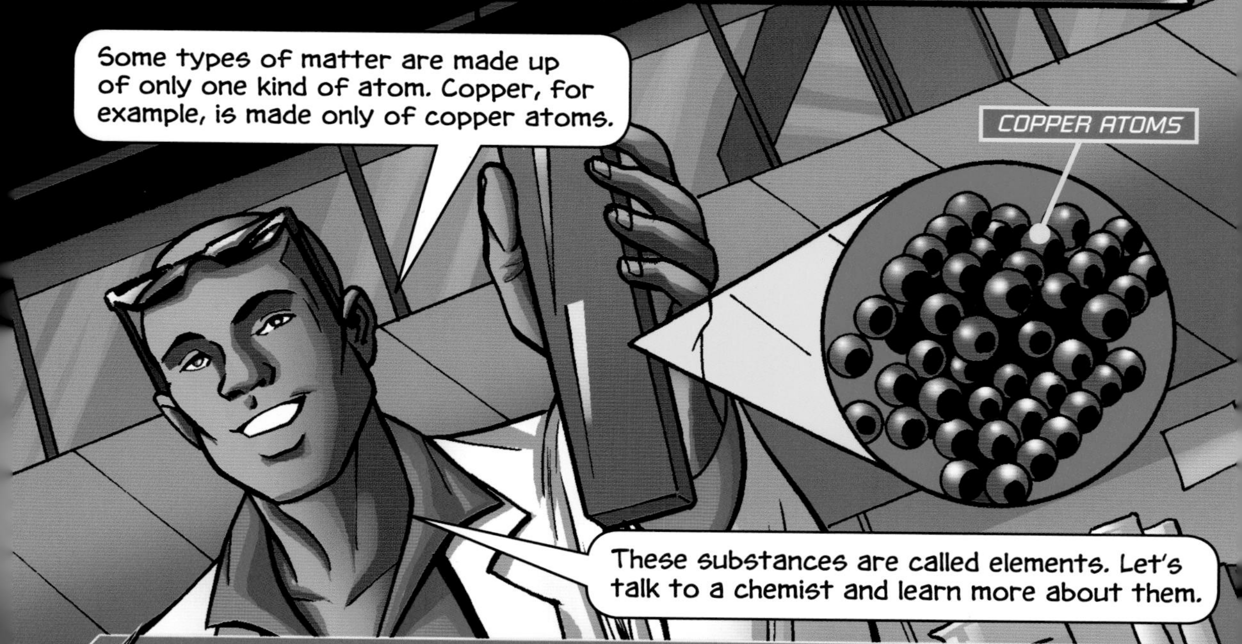
Some types of matter are made up of only one kind of atom. Copper, for example, is made only of copper atoms.
COPPER ATOMS
These substances are called elements. Let's talk to a chemist and learn more about them.

MOLECULES

ACCESS GRANTED: MAX AXIOM

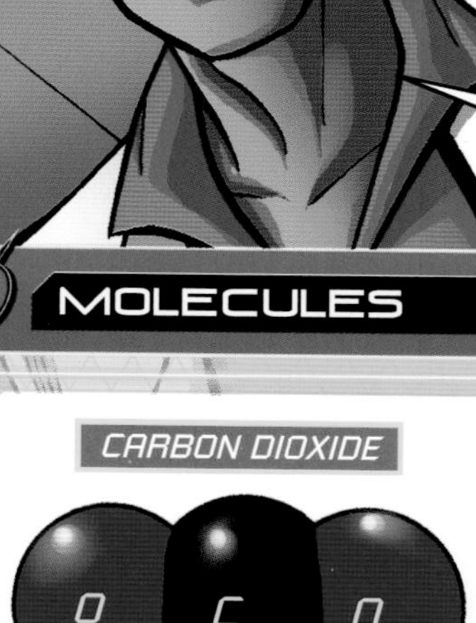
CARBON DIOXIDE
O
C
O

Molecules are made up of two or more atoms joined together. A molecule can be made up of the same or different atoms. For example, a molecule of oxygen is made up of two oxygen atoms. On the other hand, a molecule of carbon dioxide is made up of one carbon atom and two oxygen atoms.

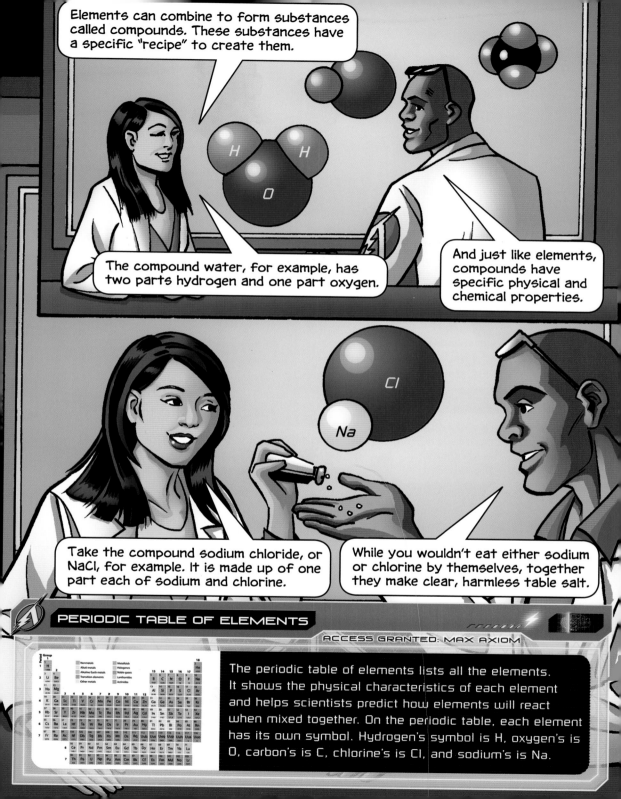

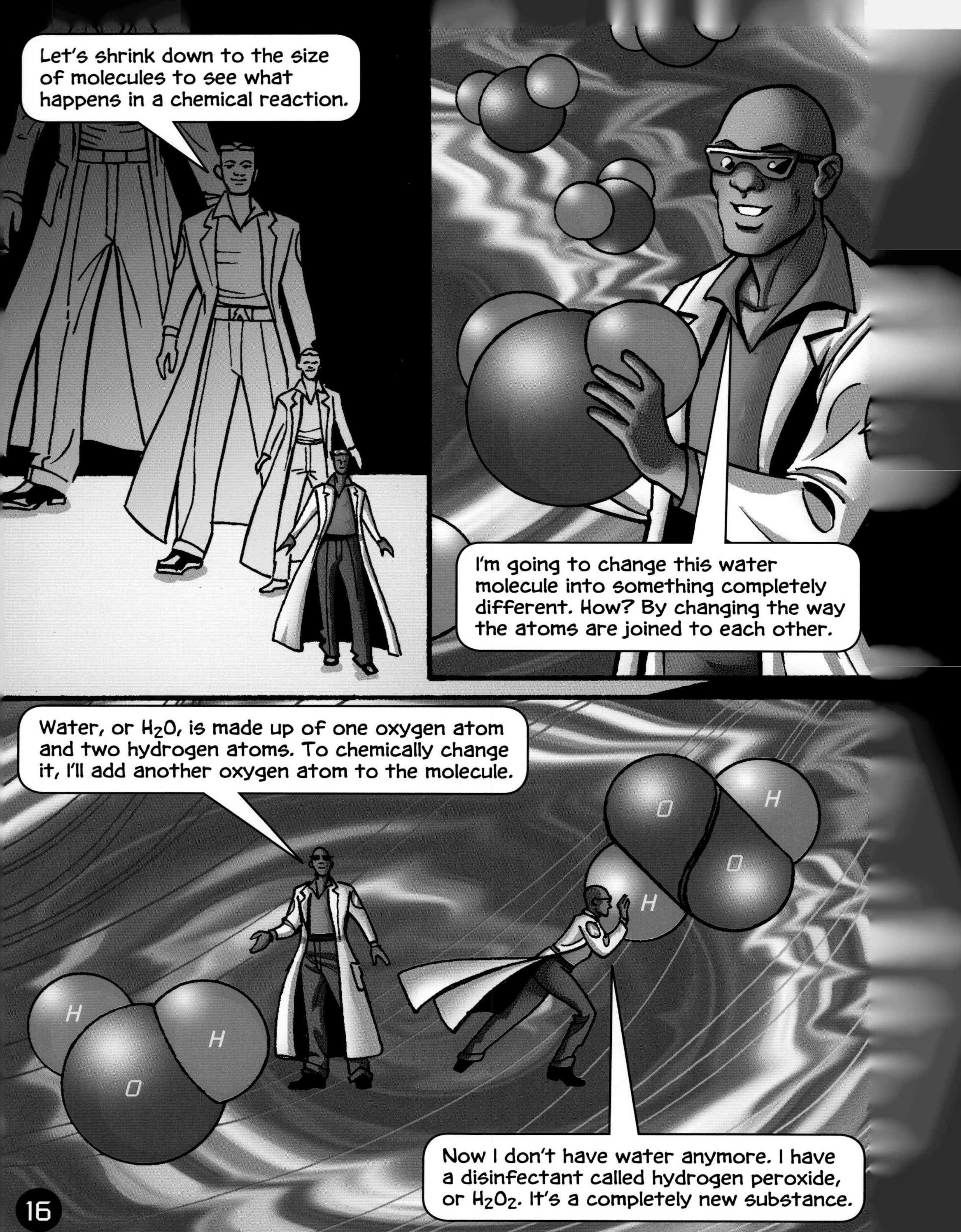
Let's shrink down to the size of molecules to see what happens in a chemical reaction.
I'm going to change this water molecule into something completely different. How? By changing the way the atoms are joined to each other.
Water, or H_2O, is made up of one oxygen atom and two hydrogen atoms. To chemically change it, I'll add another oxygen atom to the molecule.
O
H
O
H
H
H
O
Now I don't have water anymore. I have a disinfectant called hydrogen peroxide, or H_2O_2. It's a completely new substance.

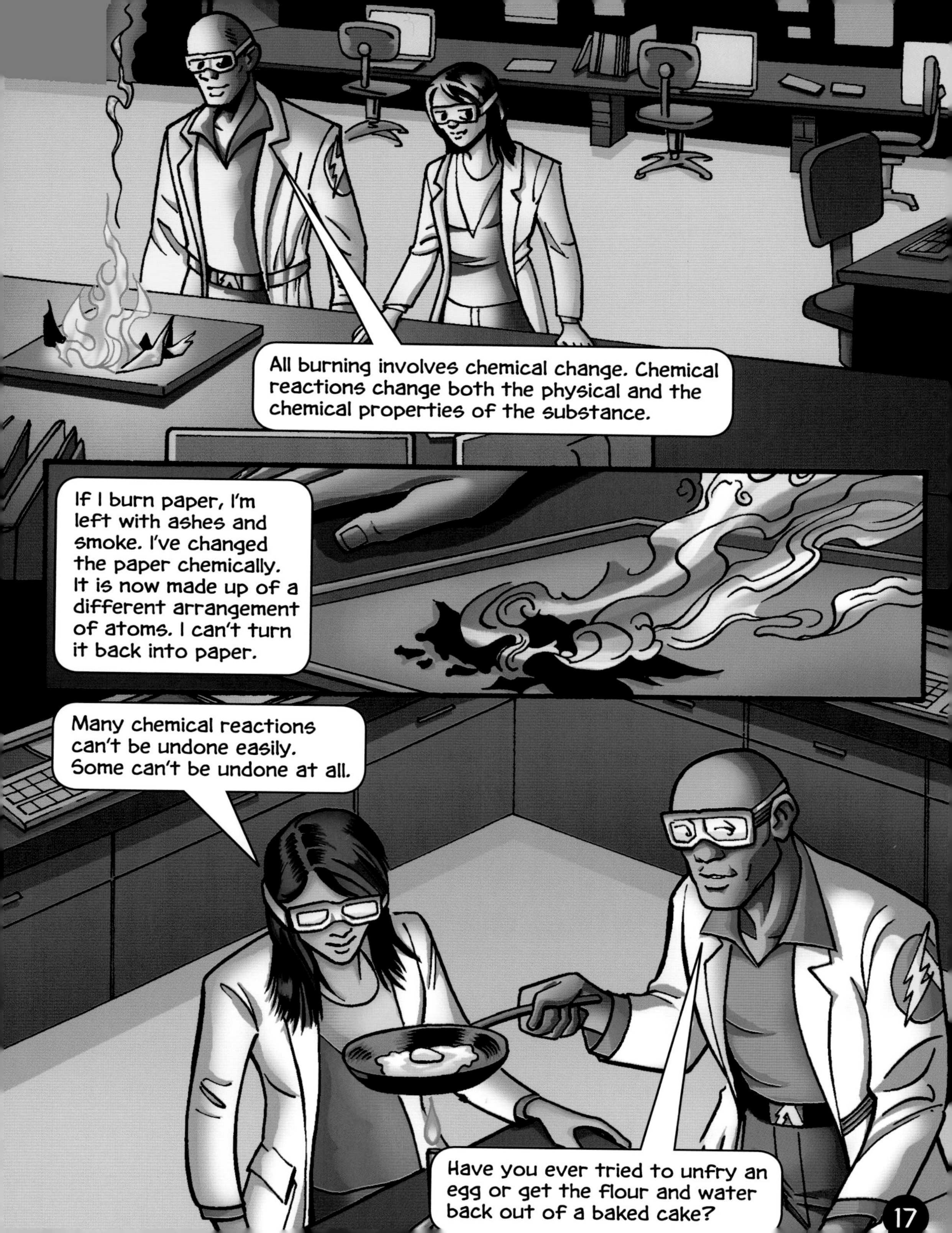
All burning involves chemical change. Chemical reactions change both the physical and the chemical properties of the substance.
If I burn paper, I'm left with ashes and smoke. I've changed the paper chemically. It is now made up of a different arrangement of atoms. I can't turn it back into paper.
Many chemical reactions can't be undone easily. Some can't be undone at all.
Have you ever tried to unfry an egg or get the flour and water back out of a baked cake?

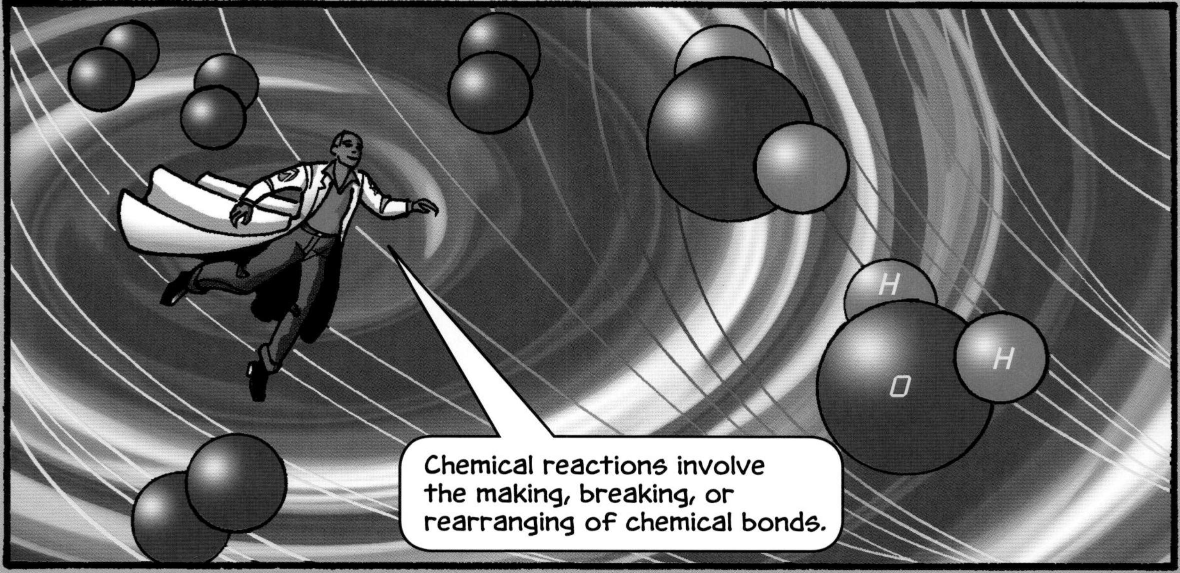
H
H
O
Chemical reactions involve the making, breaking, or rearranging of chemical bonds.

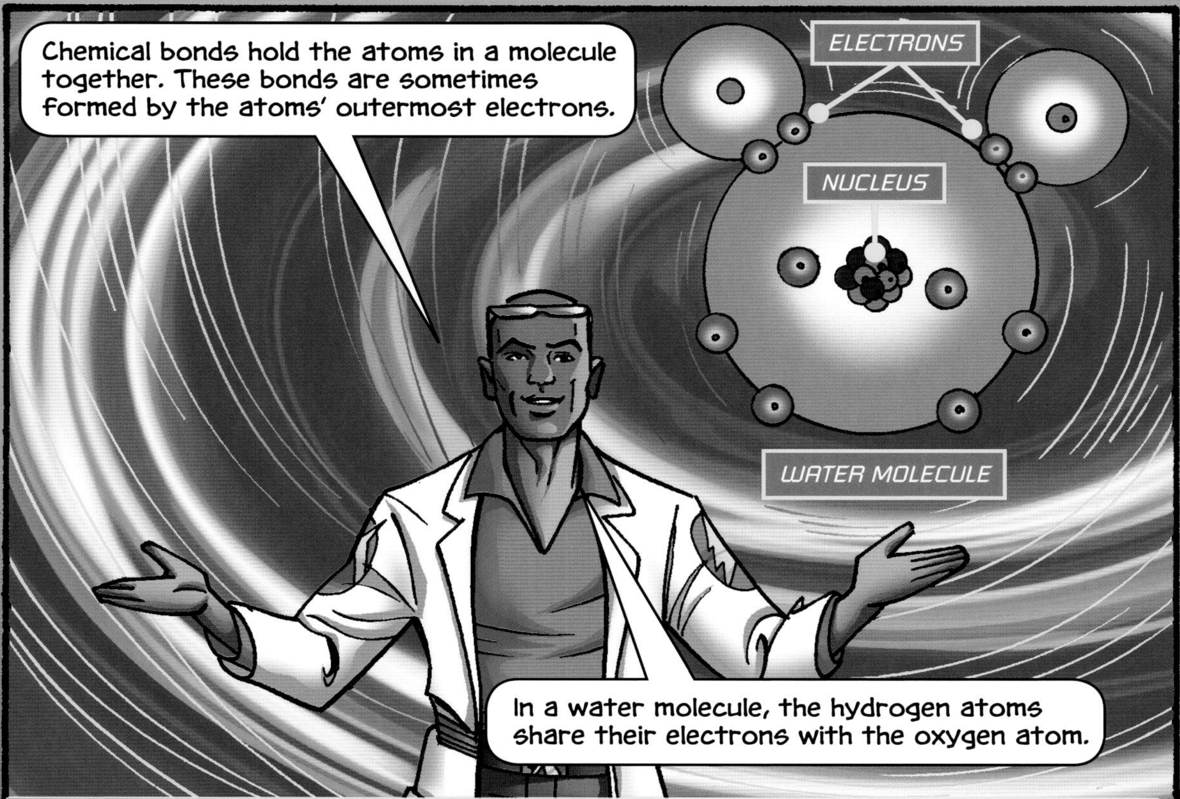
Chemical bonds hold the atoms in a molecule together. These bonds are sometimes formed by the atoms' outermost electrons.
ELECTRONS
NUCLEUS
WATER MOLECULE
In a water molecule, the hydrogen atoms share their electrons with the oxygen atom.

REACTANTS AND PRODUCTS

In a chemical reaction, the substances that undergo a chemical change are called the reactants. The substances that result from the change are called the products.

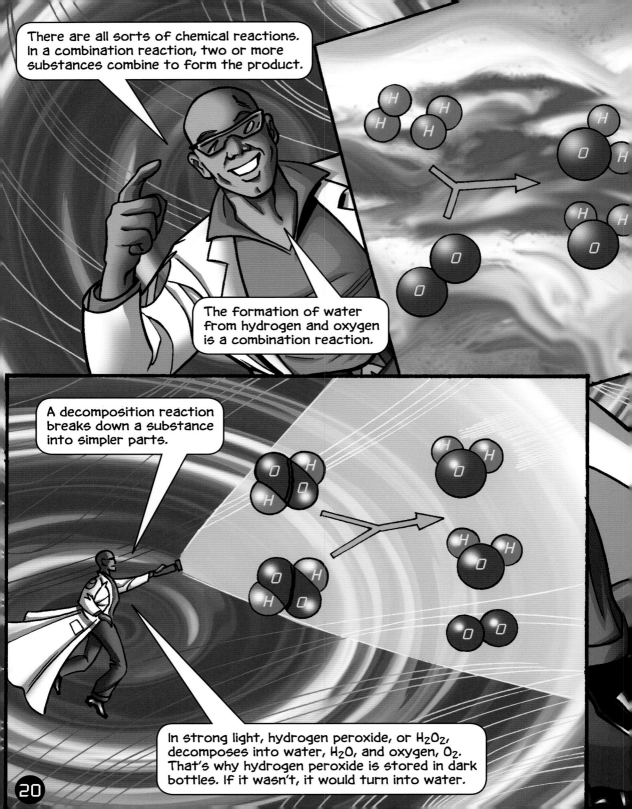

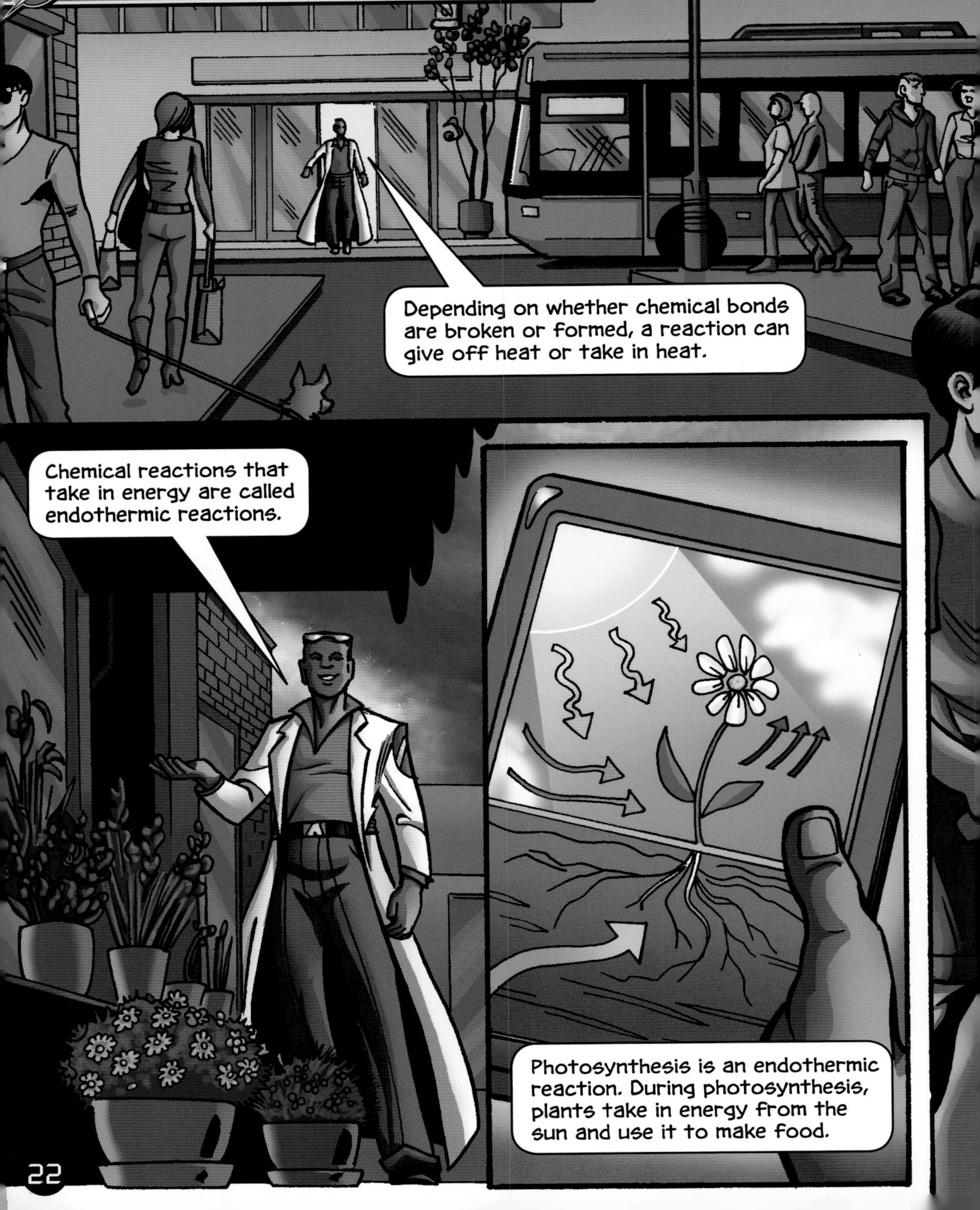
Depending on whether chemical bonds are broken or formed, a reaction can give off heat or take in heat.
Chemical reactions that take in energy are called endothermic reactions.
Photosynthesis is an endothermic reaction. During photosynthesis, plants take in energy from the sun and use it to make food.

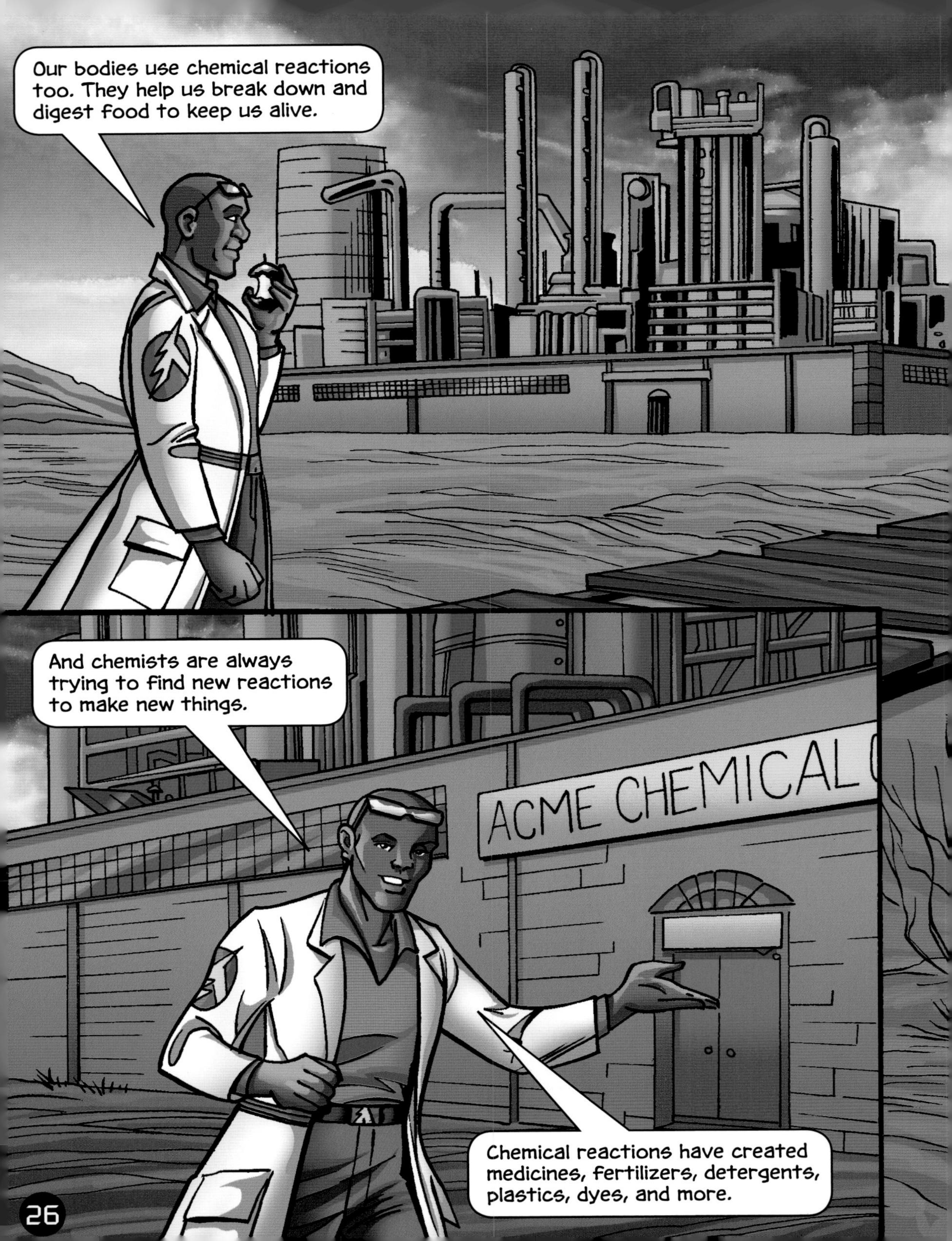
Our bodies use chemical reactions too. They help us break down and digest food to keep us alive.
And chemists are always trying to find new reactions to make new things.
ACME CHEMICAL
Chemical reactions have created medicines, fertilizers, detergents, plastics, dyes, and more.

Elements are the simplest forms of matter. There are 117 known elements in the universe. About 90 of these elements are found naturally on Earth or in the atmosphere. The others have been created in laboratories. Scientists are still working on discovering new elements.

A molecular formula tells you the total number and kinds of atoms in a molecule. Water's molecular formula is H_2O. That means to make a molecule of water you need two atoms of hydrogen (H) and one atom of oxygen (O). Carbon dioxide's formula is CO_2. That means you'd need one atom of carbon (C) and two of oxygen (O) to make a carbon dioxide molecule.

Fireflies glow because of a special reaction involving oxygen atoms and two other chemicals. The chemical reaction takes place in the firefly's abdomen. The light produced shines right through its body.

Heating chemical compounds produces the beautiful colors you see in fireworks. When heated, the compounds give off colors. To get blue, fireworks experts add copper compounds. To get orange, they add calcium.

New York's Statue of Liberty is green thanks to chemical reactions. Made of copper, the statue was originally the color of a penny. But over the years, the copper has reacted with oxygen in the air, or oxidized, to form the statue's famous green coating.

Have you ever made a volcano using baking soda and vinegar? The resulting "lava" is made by a chemical reaction. The baking soda and vinegar react to produce water, sodium acetate, and lots of fizzy carbon dioxide gas.

 Acid rain is caused by sulfur dioxide and nitrogen oxides that are released into the atmosphere by human pollution or natural events. These chemicals react with water, oxygen, and other compounds to form acid rain. Acid rain has harmful effects on the environment, wildlife, and humans.

MORE ABOUT

SUPER SCIENTIST

Real name: **Maxwell J. Axiom**
Hometown: **Seattle, Washington**
Height: **6' 1"**   Weight: **192 lbs**
Eyes: **Brown**   Hair: **None**

Super capabilities: Super intelligence; able to shrink to the size of an atom; sunglasses give x-ray vision; lab coat allows for travel through time and space.

Origin: Since birth, Max Axiom seemed destined for greatness. His mother, a marine biologist, taught her son about the mysteries of the sea. His father, a nuclear physicist and volunteer park ranger, schooled Max on the wonders of earth and sky.

One day on a wilderness hike, a megacharged lightning bolt struck Max with blinding fury. When he awoke, Max discovered a newfound energy and set out to learn as much about science as possible. He traveled the globe earning degrees in every aspect of the field. Upon his return, he was ready to share his knowledge and new identity with the world. He had become Max Axiom, Super Scientist.

Glossary

atom (AT-uhm)—an element in its smallest form

combination reaction (kom-buh-NAY-shuhn ree-AK-shuhn)—a chemical reaction where two substances combine to form a new product

combustion (kuhm-BUS-chuhn)—the process of catching fire and burning

compound (KOM-pound)—something formed by combining two or more parts

decomposition reaction (dee-kom-poh-ZIH-shuhn ree-AK-shuhn)—a chemical reaction where a substance breaks down into simpler parts

electron (i-LEK-tron)—a tiny particle in an atom that travels around the nucleus

element (E-luh-muhnt)—a basic substance in chemistry that cannot be broken down into simpler substances under ordinary lab conditions

endothermic reaction (en-doh-THUR-mic ree-AK-shuhn)—a chemical reaction that takes in energy

exothermic reaction (eks-oh-THUR-mic ree-AK-shuhn)—a chemical reaction that gives off energy

fermentation (fur-men-TAY-shuhn)—a chemical change that makes the sugar in a substance change into alcohol

matter (MAT-ur)—anything that has weight and takes up space

molecule (MOL-uh-kyool)—two or more atoms of the same or different elements that have bonded; a molecule is the smallest part of a substance that can't be divided without a chemical change

READ MORE

Brent, Lynnette. *Chemical Changes.* Why Chemistry Matters. New York: Crabtree Publishing Company, 2009.

Hoffman, Mary Ann. *Scientific Inquiry in Action: Chemical Reaction!* Science Scope. New York: PowerKids Press, 2009.

Lew, Kristi. *Chemical Reactions.* Essential Chemistry. New York: Chelsea House Publishers, 2008.

Oxlade, Chris. *Material Changes and Reactions.* Chemicals in Action. Chicago: Heinemann Library, 2007.

Solway, Andrew. *From Gunpowder to Laser Chemistry: Discovering Chemical Reactions.* Chain Reactions. Chicago: Heinemann Library, 2007.

INTERNET SITES

FactHound offers a safe, fun way to find Internet sites related to this book. All of the sites on FactHound have been researched by our staff.

Here's all you do:

Visit *www.facthound.com*

Type in this code: 9781429647724

INDEX